I0157593

activating
your God-given
potential
while young

Buhle Dlamini

young*AND*able

activating
your God-given
potential
while young

This Book is produced by
Young & Able Youth Advisory Services cc
www.youngable.com

Visit the site for more information about:

- books,
- Youth Workshops,
- Online Newsletters,
- Audio books on tape or CD
- Online Courses
- And MUCH more!

"SUCCESS IS MY CHOICE"
Postnet Suite # 4, Private Bag X03
Southdale, 2135
Johannesburg, South Africa
Web: www.youngable.com
Email: info@youngable.com

This Book is dedicated to Stacey,
my wonderful wife,
My Mother and Father,
who have both passed on,
My Grandmother, Grace Khumalo,
who has been a pillar in my life,
My Family, My In-laws, My Friends
and All those who have encouraged
me to be all I can be.

I love you and I thank God for you -
you all make my life complete!

My journey to activating my potential has been quite a ride. I am now 27 years old and I feel like one who has had a full life. That is what happens if you activate your potential while you are still young; you gain a life of significance.

I am thankful to a great number of people who have come into my life and recognised what God has planted in me. I grew up in a rural village of Hlabisa in KwaZulu-Natal in South Africa as one of umpteen children my Grandmother had to raise. Those formative years in the malnourished village made me into the man I am today. My Grandmother stands out in my memory as a woman of prayer and unshakable faith which she passed on to us. Activating my potential was a result of people who believed there was something more to the young boy without shoes and ashy knees. In essence, it was those people who saw a king inside a boy, like God saw in David.

Life is never predictable and one cannot be sure of the circumstances life will bring. What matters most is the clarity of direction and having dreams that one can realistically pursue. My rural school had very limited resources. The first library I had access to was in my Grade 8 class and it was one cupboard of books in the teachers' staff room. I still remember the excitement of getting out my first book from that library. Sadly, not many of my peers at my school took that advantage. In many ways that one cupboard library experience broadened my mind to the many possibilities I have pursued.

Now when I look back at the years that followed this is what I see: I have travelled to many places around the world. I've had numerous opportunities to impact other young people's lives in different countries. I found my true love (Stacey) as far away as Canada and married her. I built my own company Young and Able cc, authored two books – Make a Difference Generation and Godly Generation - and I speak at numerous Corporate Events in South Africa. Yet my dreams for the future are still bigger and bolder than before, because potential always has a potential to grow.

I wish both my parents had lived to see these days but I am thankful to them and to God for giving me life and a head start in the world.

Whoever picks up this book has a history but that history should never hinder your potential. I invite you to take a journey with me into your potential and change your future today - one choice at a time. It is all up to you and your faith in turning the impossible to possibilities.

2007

contents

activating your potential

H ave you ever felt like you are missing something? Felt like there is more to you than you are experiencing now?

That is because there is more to you than you are currently experiencing. There is a greater potential placed by God within each and every one of us. As much as we hear about all this potential most of us ask ourselves where this great potential is? Why am I not living up to it yet? Why am I struggling from day to day? The thing is this great potential within us, like anything worth having, needs to be activated. The potential within us will only become a reality when we get serious about taking hold of that which Christ used to take hold of us. It will not automatically fall into our laps, neither is it instant like the many things we find on the supermarket shelves today. Are you serious about living up to your God-given potential? Then it is time you did something to activate it. In this book you have 20 chapters to learn and put into action things you need to know and do about activating your potential. So I pass the challenge to you: God's part was to put this great potential in you; your part and mine is to activate it.

CHAPTER 1

understand
your maker

Why did God create me? Why am I here? Is there a reason I am here? Is it just a coincidence? Many people today will tell you many things, some will tell you about reincarnation, some will tell you we are all just a result of nature and lifecycle. This is the fundamental part of activating your potential - understanding your maker and why He created you. Think about this verse below for a moment.

> "You made all the delicate, inner parts of my body, and knit them together in my mother's womb...Your workmanship is marvelous...You were there while I was being formed....You saw me before I was born and scheduled each day of my life before I began to breathe" (Psalm 139:13-16 TLB).

You and I were designed according to plan. Nothing was left to chance. There was no photocopying when we were made, just all custom designs by a sovereign hand of God. That should tell you something about our maker; not only did he take time to make us but wrote out a plan for our lives before we even started breathing.

God created each one of us for a purpose and that purpose can only be fulfilled if we are in complete union with him. When God made us, he knew the plans he had for us, plans to give us a hope and a future (Jeremiah 29:11). And to live up to that plan we need to know Him and get with the program.

Most of us are drifting aimlessly until we submit our lives back to God and allow Him to be in the driver's seat. Before we give ourselves completely to God we are like a ship without a sailor. You see the problem with a ship without a sailor is that with every wind that blows the ship changes course and the ship keeps going but without a destination, except for destruction. A life that is not headed in the God-given direction is just an accident waiting to happen. By getting serious about our relationship with God we start our road to activating our potential. The longer we delay the process and experience of knowing God for ourselves, the longer it will be for us to realize our potential.

WHAT CAN I LEARN AND APPLY?:

understand
who you are

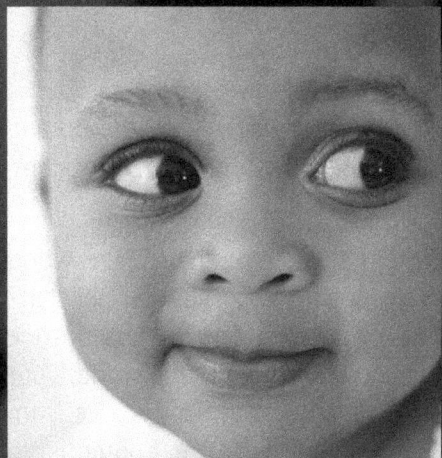

On day one we look at how you and I were designed according to plan. Nothing was left to chance. You are uniquely made, not one person in the whole world is like you. You are one of a kind and there will never be another like you.

How sad it is that many people today look at themselves and see nothing but a complete mistake. What's more sad is that even though God spent so much time making each person unique, the majority of us spend most of our time trying to be the same as the next person. Instead of spending our time trying to measure up to someone else's idea of how we should be and act; why not find out who we really are and what that means for us and about our future. Check the verse below:

" For we are God's workmanship created in Christ Jesus to do good works, which God prepared in advance for us to do." Ephesians 2:10 (NIV)

We are God's masterpieces, as some versions put it. That means God is proud of who He made us to be. He knows exactly why he made you and what He desires you to do. You are not just here by some cosmic accident, you did not just find yourself on planet earth.

You are part of plan; you fit in the great scheme of things. The world wouldn't be quite the same if you were not here. Do you believe that? It's true sometimes you may feel that if you were not in class no-one would notice. Or you may feel that if you were not in this world, your family, your community wouldn't miss you very much. This is a lie from the pit of hell. This kind of thinking causes people with great potential to pass through this world without contributing their share. They go to the grave still carrying all the potential within them without ever making any difference that counts. You have much more to contribute to this world, much more than you now realize.

The verse above goes on to say we are "created in Christ Jesus to do good works, which God prepared in advance for us to do". This means God has a purpose for creating you. You are here to do something, to fulfill your calling that God already prepared for you from the beginning. You are not a mistake, a misfit or a loser; those are the names the devil wants you to believe you are. You are God's Masterpiece, God is proud of you.

Are you constantly trying to fit into other people's views of you?

Are you happy with who and what God made you?

Looking at yourself the way God looks at you will take you a long way to living your potential.

> **"God doesn't want us just to know who we are in Him;
> He wants us to become it." Dr Myles Munroe.**

Become more and more of who you really are by knowing the truth about yourself and living up to that truth.

WHAT CAN I LEARN AND APPLY?:

take
responsibility
for your life

We live in the blame generation. When something goes wrong we look for someone to blame. We have become so good at blaming others and circumstances for everything that happens that we never take any responsibility. We create reasons why we are not living to our full potential so that we can hide behind these facades and never take responsibility.

It is much easier to blame our parents, our teachers and our society than to stand up and fight for our God-given potential. God planted potential in you for the benefit of the world and yourself in fulfilling His purpose. You are responsible for making sure that this potential is activated and that you live up to what God meant you to become. Start taking responsibility for your life now while you are young so that you will be all that you can be.

Listen to Paul's instruction to young Timothy:

> **"Don't let anyone look down on you because you are young, but set an example for the believers in speech, in life, in love, in faith and in purity." 1 Timothy 4:12**

Start taking responsibility for your future. Not only that, but also become an example to others while you are at it. How you live your life will say a lot about your future. Starts realizing that your future depends on what you do with your life now. The decisions you make today will determine the kind of future you will have tomorrow.

Think about the things that will contribute positively to your future. Timothy was told that he should set an example; the same applies to you. Instead of blaming your parents or people around you for influencing you badly, be a good influence on them. Look at your life, the way you speak, the way you love and your faith in God. In these areas, who is in control?

Is it other people and circumstances or is it you by God's Spirit who is in control? When you watch TV who is in control? When you hang out with your friends; who is in control of your tongue? When it comes to managing your time; who is in control?

You cannot blame other people about your future. Sure enough circumstances and your background can definitely make it hard for you sometimes but ultimately God wants you to take responsibility of those things you can. Many people have risen from horrible backgrounds and became pillars of society and contributed greatly to the world. They all took responsibility for their lives and with God's help continued to live successful lives. If you want to activate your potential you have got to stop the blame game and look within.

What areas are you still struggling with now? Do you continue to do things you know you shouldn't? Are you committed to put an end to laziness, procrastination (putting things off and never getting to do them) and following the wrong crowd etc? Get with the program or be left behind. I encourage you to think deeply about this and then act.

WHAT CAN I LEARN AND APPLY?:

deal
with the past

Our past, if we allow it, can be a huge hindrance in us realizing and fulfilling our God-given potential. Countless people who have not achieved very much with their lives can tell you exactly why they never did. Reasons include: "My parents were poor", "I wasn't smart at school", "My father was abusive", "I was never given a chance" - the list can go on.

The issues of our past are real and as intimidating as anything. Unless they are dealt with and conquered, they can have such a hold on our lives that they hinder our development.

Think of your own past. What sorts of issues confront you as you seek to move forward - the background of inadequate education, a broken family, abuse, poverty? Whatever it is, it's real, but it can also be overcome with God's help. God holds the key. He is the one able to heal and change situations. Find out what in your past is holding you back and once you have done that, ask God to help you deal with it and overcome it. If you can't do it alone talk to someone who can help you. Find a counsellor and seek help but don't just sit with it.

In all of this it is important to note that we should never allow ourselves to be victims of our past. We can use the hardships of our past to be the stepping-stones for our future. One person that did that in our country is our former State President Nelson Mandela - not only did he use his hardships as stepping stones, he never allowed himself to be a victim.

Our past doesn't only hold the things that happened to us but it also holds the things we have done. Maybe you carry a certain label based on something you did. When you rock up at the local hang out people start to whisper "here comes a thief, a drug addict, an alcoholic" and so on.

"If we confess our sins, he (God) is faithful and just and will forgive us our sins and purify us from all unrighteousness." 1 John 1:9

Make sure that you have set your record straight with God and those you might have offended, then God promises to wipe the slate clean. God always gives us another chance it is up to us to take that chance.

Rahab, was one woman who could be ashamed of her past, she was a prostitute. But when an opportunity to live for God came she took it, we read about her in Joshua 2:1-22. When the Israelite spies came to her land, she believed in their God and hid them and secured safety for herself and her family when God gave victory to Israel over Jericho. She went on to become the mother of Boaz and was part of the lineage from which Jesus was born (Matthew 1:5). She did not allow her past to hinder God's plan for her life.

Never let where you have been, what you used to be or what you have done prevent you from being what you were meant to be.

WHAT CAN I LEARN AND APPLY?:

_____

_____

_____

_____

_____

_____

_____

_____

_____

_____

_____

_____

_____

_____

_____

_____

_____

_____

deal
with the
critics

One of the biggest reasons many people never live up to their dreams and potential is the negative and cynical attitudes of other people. We grow up in a world which conditions young people to base their decisions on what other people think.

Daily we are manipulated by thoughts such as: "What will others say if I decide to do this?" "What if others laugh at me?" It is usually the people closest to us that can hinder us by their attitudes.

Family, friends, teachers, fellow workers, boyfriends and girlfriends are those people. Family and friends can kill our dreams and our pursuits to our true potential if we let them. People will always be ready to tell us what we can and cannot do. Most times it's not even done in words but with a look, a cynical smile and a lot of other negative vibrations. It is much easier for others to point out the obstacles, and give reasons why we cannot do what we are attempting to do.

Joseph had a dream (Genesis 37) at the age of 17, and the bible tells us that when he told his brothers, they hated him even more. (CONTEXT?)

You might have been broken by destructive words spoken over your life by people who didn't know your royal heritage – God has a destiny for you.

> **"But you are a chosen people, a royal priesthood, a holy nation, a people belonging to God, that you may declare the praises of him who called you out of darkness into light." 1Peter 2:9**

People around us don't always catch on to the potential God has placed in us and when we share our dreams with them they can easily put us down without even knowing it. If you listen to and believe everything people say about you or to you, you can miss out on what is planned for you. Sometimes people can be threatened by what God has for us if they are not pursuing their own God-given potential.

Believe in a God of unlimited potential who continues to empower people to reach their dreams. Stay away from negative people who crush your dreams and keep company with other dreamers. Stay dedicated to the belief that you have unlimited potential and to the dreams that God has given you.

This can sometimes be a final straw to block you from your God-given potential. It will take determination to rise above the negative responses that come from others. Maybe people have said to you that you'll never amount to anything, that you're not smart enough that you are ugly etc. If you allow what they say to determine your future you'll always confirm their predictions over your life.

Decide today to deal with other people's expectations of you in a proper manner. Remember that your destiny is dependent on God working through you and not others.

Take time to think about how you have stopped pursuing some dreams because of something that someone did or said. Choose to reclaim all your dreams not relying on people's criticism but on what God has told you. *Do not allow all that potential that has been entrusted to you to waste away because of what others have said or have done to you. The choice is always yours.*

WHAT CAN I LEARN AND APPLY?:

grasping
your purpose

What is purpose? Purpose speaks about the reason for existence. For something to exist there must be a reason, a function that it fulfils. The purpose of a kettle is to boil water so we can enjoy tea. The kettle's main reason for existence is to boil water - it wasn't meant for cooking or watering flowers.

Just like a kettle has a specific purpose for being what it is, you also have a purpose and a reason for being you.

Realizing your God-given purpose is the key to activating and living up to your God-given potential. When we are born or growing up, no-one knows which one of us is going to be the president, the soccer star, the gifted artist, the successful businessman, the great doctor and the powerful evangelist.

Purpose is born out of dreams, aspirations and desires, which are planted by God the Holy Spirit in us. Take a look at the story of Joseph from Genesis 37. As a young boy there was no way of knowing what God's purpose/plan for Joseph was, just like it is with all of us. There is no way of knowing unless we start to follow our God given dreams.

> **Joseph did dream: Genesis 37:5 "Joseph had a dream, and when he told it to his brothers they hated him even more."**

We read earlier that God created us, and it is God who gives us dreams that we can pursue for our lives. I am not talking about selfish dreams or dreams that come from selfish motives. I am, however, talking about dreams that make us a people with purpose a people who desire and want to make a difference.

Martin Luther King Jnr had a dream, a vision of a better future where people would not be judged by the colour of their skins but by the content of their character. He had a dream that things could be better than they were then and to this dream he devoted his life and even lost his life to that dream. I believe that Martin Luther King Jnr discovered his life purpose through that dream and his life was shaped by that purpose.

God is ready to reveal his purpose for your life, but you need to be willing to have God embed his dream (his purpose) within you. God can do it in these ways:

- **Damascus Road experience (Acts 9:3-16) where God reveals his purpose for you in a bold and supernatural way.**

- **Growing realization of what you are meant to do as you get closer and closer to him.**

- **You see the need, and you know you're called to meet it and something clicks within you.**

As you discover God's will for your life you will see that your skills, talents and characteristics have been given in line with that purpose. You have to discover for yourself what God designed you to do.

What dreams has God planted in you? The Holy Spirit is there to help you in this process.

"For it is God who works in you to will and to act according to his good purpose." Philippians 2:13.

When God made you, He had a unique purpose for your life in mind. Discover it!

WHAT CAN I LEARN AND APPLY?:

understand your potential

We keep coming back to the same statement as we go through this topic. God has planted great potential in each and every one of us. What do we mean by potential? My Dictionary puts it this way:

POTENTIAL- *The Inherent Capacity for Growth or Development*

Capable Of Being But Not Yet In Existence

Potential is what might be, what could be, but isn't yet and we all possess it. Potential is about what great achievements that lie dormant, untapped and unrealized within each and every one of us. There is, however a huge difference between having potential and fulfilling that potential. A huge number of people in the world live way below their potential and because they have not connected with their purpose die with all that potential still untapped and unrealized.

> **"If we all did the things we are capable of we would literary astound ourselves." Thomas Edison**

> **"I can do all things through Christ Jesus who gives me strength" Philippians 4:13**

There is no limit to what we can do through Christ except the limitations we put on ourselves. David would have never realized his potential to defeat Goliath the giant had he not activated that potential through his faith in God.

Moses would never have realized his potential to lead a nation out of bondage had he not trusted God and did what no man had ever done before.

To understand and live up to your potential means that you will not be satisfied with an average life. God did not create you to be average. He did not create you to just get by making a living; but he created you to be a winner and a conqueror. Your potential is closely linked to the power of God that lives in you. The power of God in you is not average but extraordinary and supernatural.

What limitations have you put to your God-given potential?

Undermining your potential undermines the one who created you and made his power available to you. Imagine an eagle with an ability to fly above the clouds but always flies with the pigeons. How much energy and power is wasted by this eagle as it gets by with as little as possible?

We miss out on a lot when we do not discover the great power that God has placed in us. Believe that God can do much more through you as you realize your God-given potential.

WHAT CAN I LEARN AND APPLY?:

CHAPTER 8

conditions
to your
potential

Available for groups
of 3 or 4 travelling
to or from Tsing Yi
or Kowloon Station

There are all kinds of products that are on sale out there. TV adverts tell you of a product that allows you to eat all the bad food you want to eat and still lose weight. In today's world people want to live unhealthy lives and still remain healthy. Some people want to remain lazy but still earn a lot of money, and as a result there are many scams out there that promise to make people rich by doing nothing.

This is not what realizing your potential is about. If you are to become a young man or woman that God created you to be, you need to understand the conditions that are tied to it. Every action you take has a result and living your potential is greatly dependent on the actions you take. As you sow, so shall you reap. You cannot expect grapes from an apple tree. Mushrooms only grow in damp, dark places and certain fruits only grow in tropical conditions.

There needs to be certain factors that are just right and conducive for your potential to be released. Some people ignore these conditions and enjoy temporary success.

"What good is it for a man to gain the whole world, and yet lose or forfeit his own life?" Luke 9:25

"Do not be conformed to the standards of this world any longer but be transformed by the renewing of your mind. Then you will be able to test and approve what God's will is – his good, pleasing and perfect will." Romans 12:2

To know and live up to God's will for your life you can no longer think the same way as the world thinks. Something has got to change about the way you see the world. Your standards can't be the same as that of the world but become higher as you allow God to transform your mind.

Your motives need to change to fit that which is pleasing to God. Your lifestyle needs to reflect that of a child of God. God can change us from being self-centered people who only care about self to be people who are concerned about others and the world around us.

What areas have you not yet submitted to God about your life?

Is it pride, jealousy, selfishness, godless language, anger, sexual immorality etc?

You will never fully experience God's best for you if you hold on to these things. If you want God to fill your hands with treasures that he has for you, you've got to let go of the rubbish you are clutching in your hands.

The Devil will do anything to keep you holding on to these things. But God will transform you by the renewing of your mind as you allow the Holy Spirit to work in your life.

Take time to identify some areas where you are still conforming to this world and ask God to transform your mind today. Remember that every decision that you take has a direct impact on your potential and your future.

WHAT CAN I LEARN AND APPLY?:

the character test

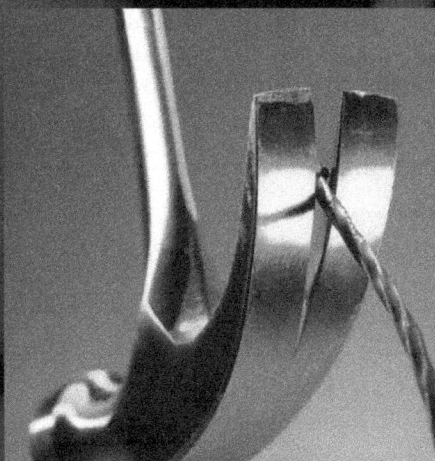

The testing of your character comes before the fulfillment of your dreams and potential. What do you understand about character? When people speak of someone as being a person of character, what do they mean?

Character in a biblical sense is tied in with moral virtue; God's standard of behavior and a lifestyle that sets you apart from the crowd. A person of character will be a person that demonstrates these features in their day-to-day life.

Character is not something you put on and off but is part of who you are. And you become who you are because of the choices you make. There are a lot of young people who are not what they were created to be because of the choices they have made. God didn't create anybody to be a thief, a prostitute or a murderer rather the choices these people have made have led them to where they are.

No matter how difficult your background may be, you still have a choice about what character you want to develop. Character is very important in activating your potential because God won't entrust you with his gifts and blessings before you are ready to handle them.

Take a look at the story of Joseph from Genesis 37. Read this story and see if you can identify the following areas of character-building that Joseph had to go through.

Firstly, let us look at what God's dream or God's purpose was for Joseph. According to the dreams God gave Joseph, he was called to be greater than his brothers while his family would need his help to survive in the future. Joseph was destined for greatness and would be able to use his position to help others. This was God's plan for Joseph.

But Joseph's character needed some work to start with. He was a spoiled brat; he bragged about his dreams and was full of pride. This was not a character of a man God wanted Joseph to be. The same can apply to us when we start out we can be full of ourselves and proud' yet on the other hand we can think so low of our abilities and ourselves. Both of these attitudes are not right. Character is molded through tough circumstances. How we respond to these circumstances will determine the character we acquire as a result.

In Joseph's case these circumstances meant being sold to slavery, facing temptation and being thrown into jail wrongfully. Joseph's response to these tests to his character was working hard, being faithful, going the extra mile and using his gifts. Joseph's character was built through the tests that he endured and his response to these led to him fulfilling his purpose and living his potential.

For us to fulfill our potential we need to pass the tests that come our way. It all boils down to being faithful to what God has given you.

"Whoever is faithful with very little can also be trusted with much... so if you are not trustworthy with worldly wealth, who will trust you with true riches?" Luke 16:10-11

Being a person of character is not easy, but it is the key to you activating your potential. Do you respond to challenges with hard work, faithfulness, going the extra mile, using your gifts for good works and not bad?

Think about the hardships you face even now. How will you respond? Will you be like Joseph and show God and others you can be trusted to do the right thing even if it is hard? Your answers to these questions will shape the character you are going to have. Decide now what kind of character you want to possess, write it down and always weigh your responses to that.

WHAT CAN I LEARN AND APPLY?:

battling
for your
dream

Fulfilling your God-given purpose and living up to your potential will often require you to battle for the dream God has for you. You must be prepared to fight for the vision that God gives you.

Nelson Mandela had to battle for the dream that he had of a free South Africa where everyone was equal. In his Rivonia Trial speech prior to being thrown into prison for 27 years he said:

> **"I have fought against white domination; I have fought against black domination; during my lifetime I have cherished an ideal of a free society. It is an ideal for which I hope to live for, and if needs be, it is an ideal for which I am prepared to die."**

> **Martin Luther King, JNR, said:**

> **"I submit to you that if a man hasn't discovered something that he will die for, he isn't fit to live." Martin Luther King, JNR, did die for his dream and the fruits of his dream many still enjoy today.**

From both of these great leaders who lived out their potential, we learn that if you have a dream, you must be prepared to battle for it if it's to become a reality.

In today's world of instant everything the idea that you have to fight for anything is not welcome. But we have to face this most important fact that if we want our potential to become a reality, we've got to be willing to fight for it. The bible is filled with men and women who had to fight for their dreams. God gave them a dream but he definitely didn't hand it to them on a silver platter.

Abraham was promised he would be a father of a nation but he had to wait in faith and trust God as his son was born when he was 100 years old!

David was anointed as king in his teen years and had to fight the giant, run from Saul who wanted to kill him before he finally he became a king.

There are many more characters in the bible who had to fight even though God had already given them a vision and a dream for their lives. You and I are no different, if we are to live out our potential we must be prepared to battle for our God-given dream.

Watch out for paths of artificial peace. **"And the peace of God which passes all understanding will guide your hearts and minds in Christ Jesus." Philippians 4: 6b.** Many people translate this passage of scripture to mean that following God's dream for your life means you won't have to fight. So people start to look for the route with the least resistance and translate that to being God's peace. This is an artificial path of peace.

The right path does not mean having no opposition. You may be on the right path and face opposition from people you love. Some people will not understand you but if you believe and know that this is God's dream for you, you will face anything and still have the peace from God. The peace of God does not translate to having least resistance. Satan will definitely try all his tricks to stand in your way and to convince you that the right way is the wrong way so you will settle for less.

> **"Not that I have already obtained all this, or have already been made perfect, but I press on to take hold of that for which Christ Jesus took hold of me." Phil. 3:12**

Paul understood that he had to continue to battle and press on to take hold of the dream for which Christ Jesus took hold of him. We are no different; if we are to become all that God wants us to be we have to press on even when it is hard.

Are you prepared to battle for your God-given dream?

Do you realize that it is normal for opposition to come if you are on the right track?

What are the battles you have to face right now? What is your response to them? Choose today to be willing to fight for your potential.

WHAT CAN I LEARN AND APPLY?:

the
foundation
of faith

For every human being the realm of possibility depends on each individual's ability to have faith or to believe in something.

Faith is the foundation for living a life that is fulfilled and is pleasing to God. The bible clearly states that it is impossible to please God without faith (Hebrews 11:6).

> So what is faith then? "Now faith is being sure of what we hope for and certain of what we do not see." Hebrews 11:1.

WOW! That says it all! If we are ever to realize and live out our God-given Potential, which is not yet seen, we have got to first believe that it is there. Many people will tell you that they do not believe in anything and yet they want to achieve great things. You just cannot accomplish God's best for you without faith, which is belief in the unseen. Faith is what keeps people going on their journey to fulfilling their God-given dreams and potential. In their minds they have seen the dream, the goal, the end result and so they spend their energies in turning that potential that dream to reality.

> "Everything is possible for him who believes." Mark 9:23

> Jesus replied, "Because you have so little faith. I tell you the truth, if you have faith as small as a mustard seed, you can say to this mountain, 'Move from here to there' and it will move. Nothing will be impossible for you." Matthew 17:20

Jesus made some powerful statements and they carry as much power in them now as they did when they were said more that 2000 years ago. This means that a person who truly believes will set no limits on what God can do. Go over the last sentence again let it sink. Yes, our lack of faith can set limits on what God can do as far as we are concerned and a complete belief will take away those limits.

All around the world today potential is stifled in people's lives because of their lack of faith. People have stopped believing. Things that are happening all around us have led people to stop believing in a lot of things. Many people no longer believe in government, in justice, in freedom, in happiness and indeed in God. Because of their lack of belief they miss out on so much and they put a limit to what can be possible in their lives.

What about you today? Have your past experiences of betrayal, discouragement and hardships blocked your ability to believe like a little child?

Why don't you spend time examining your faith today?

Realize that you need to believe in the impossible for you to live your potential. If your dreams don't require you to believe in what seems impossible for you now, than your dreams are not big enough.

Faith allows you to attempt the extraordinary. It allows you to really begin to tap into your unrealized potential, which can only be realized through God's power at work in you.

Dare to believe in the impossible, dare to dream bigger than your current situation, dare to have dreams that can only be achieved through God's power.

WHAT CAN I LEARN AND APPLY?:

discover
your God-given dreams

God has planted in each and every one of us desires that are in line with his purpose for our lives. Since it is God who created us, it is also him who planted desires within us that encourage us to make a difference in the world.

At one point or another, I am sure you have felt within yourself that there is something more, something bigger for you to accomplish in this world. You have felt that you can make a difference in the lives of others and that is where your purpose lies. God's purpose for you and indeed for every person is that you live such a life that will bring glory to him and make a significant difference in your world daily.

So what can the Bible tell us about our God-given desires and dreams to make a difference?

> **"Delight yourself in the Lord and he will give you the desires of your heart. Commit your ways to the Lord and trust in him." Psalm 37:4-5 (NIV)**

> **"Take delight in the Lord and he will give you your heart's desires commit everything you do to the Lord. Trust him and he will help you." Psalm 37:4-5 (NLT)**

Through these passages of scripture we learn this important truth: Our true desires are realized when we acknowledge God and put our trust in Him. You will find that when you delight yourself in the Lord, finding your joy only in doing what God the Father will have you do, he in turn will give you the true desires of your heart.

Sometimes these true desires of your heart might be hidden when you are too busy pursuing your ideas outside of God's plan. Many people who spend precious years on dreams which were never meant to be theirs to start with, find themselves dealing with a lot of heartache because they left God out of the equation.

Don't waste any more precious time on long detours that will lead you to dead ends and closed doors. Start now while you are young to seek the face of God about what he will have you do and delight yourself in that.

Many of us have lofty ideas of being pop-stars and famous Hollywood actors and actresses, while we don't even have the talent needed for such dreams. To start to live out your God-given dreams you must ask the one who made you what he equipped you for when he created you.

Spend some time today in God's presence, ask God to show you what your true desires are that he planted in you. Ask him to reveal himself to you as he did to so many others before us.

God already knows you completely so do not hesitate to trust him and what he will show you about yourself because he only wants the best for you. Believe me I know, and it is so exciting to be living out my dreams, which are in line with God's purpose for my life.

Start the process today. Ask and you shall receive, seek and you shall find, knock and the door shall be open unto you.

WHAT CAN I LEARN AND APPLY?:

your
life
purpose

Activating your potential is all about asking yourself all the right questions. Those who live out their purpose in life are the people who go out to identify it. I believe God is already showing you the desires He planted in you.

DREAMS/DESIRES
What do you really desire to do?

TALENTS/GIFTS
What are you naturally good at?

OPPORTUNITY
What opportunities are available for you?

GOD'S WILL
What does God want for your life?

Our God-given purpose lies in the tiny place where our desires, our gifts, and opportunities overlap with God's. To discover this tiny place we need to ask ourselves and answer with God's help the following questions:

What am I really good at?

What do I really desire to do with my life?

What opportunities are out there for me?

What does God want for my life?

Answering these questions honestly will lead you to the place where you'll find your God-given purpose. It is possible to convince yourself that a selfish dream is your God-given dream. You need to beware of selfish ideas which are not inline with God's values. Your God-given purpose is fully in line with God's values, which should be yours as the child of God. That is why it is so vital to keep a close relationship with God, letting him guide you with every decision you make. God will not allow you fall if you seek to do only that which he desires for you to do.

Ask God to start pruning those desires that are just selfish and not of him and ask him to show you the way you should take.

Start by answering the following questions and see how close you get to identifying your life purpose. Do not rush through this exercise it is one of the most important exercises you will do in this book. If you need to take moments by yourself where nobody will disturb you, do not hesitate. It's your life we're talking about here.

GOD'S WILL (Matthew 6:33)
What does God want for my life?

DREAMS/DESIRES (Psalm 37:4)
What do I really desire to do?

GIFTS/TALENTS

What am I naturally good at?

_____

_____

_____

_____

OPPORTUNITY

What opportunities are available for me?

_____

_____

_____

_____

WHAT CAN I LEARN AND APPLY?:

uncovering your dreams & desires

L

ook and you will find it-what is unsought will go undetected.

Sophocles

"Ask and it will be given to you; seek and you will find; knock and the door will be open to you" Matthew 7:7

As young people we often live our lives as if we are on a conveyer belt, expecting everything to just happen to us automatically one step after another. We go through school and expect to go on to university and get excellent jobs. But just in case you haven't realized, there is something wrong with conveyer belt today.

Nothing happens automatically and the old saying "Go to school, get good grades and get a nice job" no longer applies. You have to get up and seek out your dream and make it a reality, find what you do well and do it to the best of your ability. The conveyer belt is broken!

It is very important to take time to search and discover what your true God-given desires are. It is possible that due to discouragement and lack of resources at the time we bury our dreams and count them as impossible. Maybe you had a great desire to be an artist and you started painting but lacked the right tools to accomplish this and so you squashed that dream.

To dream and to have desires does not mean that you already have everything you need to accomplish that dream. The dreams and desires are just the starting point; it is where we get in touch with the purpose for which we were created. The world will miss out greatly if you never start on that path of pursuing your dreams, which God planted in you.

Firstly, God plants the dream or the desire within you, and then you need to accept that dream realizing that you don't yet have all that is needed to make it a reality.

55

A desire is something that fills you up with energy when you think about, something that gives you hope about the future and something you feel you can accomplish. Another word which can be used to describe desire is passion. We can do many things but there are few things that we do with passion and these things are where our true desires lie.

> **"If you don't know what your passion is, realize that one reason for your existence on earth is to find it."**
> **Oprah Winfrey**

Follow this simple exercise to help you start to uncover the desires and dreams that are in you.

UNCOVERING YOUR DESIRES/DREAMS
Answer the following questions as honestly as you can with a pencil. Include as many answers as you can. Spend at least 15 Minutes and do not leave out anything because it sounds stupid or impossible just be honest with yourself.

Ask yourself:

What am I passionate about and what excites me to think about?

_____

_____

_____

_____

_____

What do I really love doing and able to do?

_____

_____

_____

_____

_____

What do others often ask me to help them with?

_____

_____

_____

_____

What do I have that will benefit others around me?

_____

_____

_____

_____

As you answer these questions you will start to tap into some of your God-given desires and dreams. You will see that your answers will start to really show you some of the things you might have neglected in the past.

Ask God the Holy Spirit to reveal to your mind the things that you have long buried within your heart. Jesus teaches us to **"Knock and the door will be open unto you, seek and you shall find, ask and it will be given unto you."** Follow that advice and see God reveal to you His desires for you.

WHAT CAN I LEARN AND APPLY?:

CHAPTER 15

clarify
your values

t's not hard to make decisions when you know what your values are. – Roy Disney

"Seek first the Kingdom of God and his righteousness and all these things shall be added unto you."
Matthew 6:33

The decisions we make about life are largely influenced by the values we hold. Your values are those things that matter most to you, the things you do not negotiate. Values are developed over a period of time they are formed through a combination of our past experiences and things we have learnt over time. These values form our world view, in other words they shape how we see the world around us.

Some of the values we now carry with us are not really what God desires us to have, but because of our background these now form a part of us. God has set out vales for us in His word, which he created us to live by. These values include such things as honouring God, honesty, truth, justice and more.

So often we take it for granted that we are clear about our values until something happens which really shakes us and questions our values. Your values will form your character and influence you in the dreams you choose to pursue for your life. Take for an example, if one of your values is keeping a close relationship with God. In other words, your relationship with God is of uttermost importance to you, automatically that will cut out a lot of options that aren't pleasing to God.

In this case you wouldn't see a life as the richest drug dealer as a dream to pursue, because that will negatively impact on your relationship with God. However, if your values include making as much money as possible whatever it takes, your dreams and the decisions you'll take will be affected and you'll do things that will dishonour God.

"You cannot consistently perform in the manner which is inconsistent with yourself."

Why don't you take time today to uncover some of the values that you want to live by and see how that helps you in your journey?

Uncovering Your Values

1. List five things that you consider to be most important in life

_____

_____

_____

_____

_____

2. List four to six things you want out of life. Include things that are tangible like making money as well as intangibles such as helping others, raising a family and being a good husband, etc.

_____

_____

_____

_____

_____

_____

WHAT CAN I LEARN AND APPLY?:

developing
the little
things

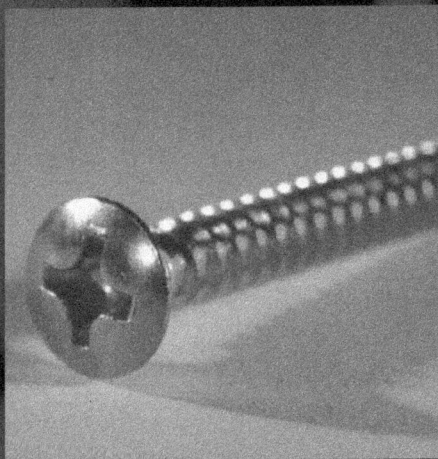

> I f I had eight hours to chop down a tree, I'd spend six sharpening my axe. - Abraham Lincoln

Isn't amazing how big things are held together by little things? If little things – such as screws in heavy machinery- are not in place they can cause big things to collapse. Big electronic machines usually depend on very tiny micro-chips without which they cannot function. All around us we see big things and we admire them and seldom do we think about the little things that make them work.

In our own lives we tend to do the same - we are always trying to develop the "big things"; things others can see and admire. As a result we fail to recognize the potential which exists in our lives because we lack the evidence of "big things" we think are so important.

Here is a trick you need to learn early if you are to activate your potential: the big oak tree is in the acorn, a field of grain is in the seed. This is how God works in all things; when you pray for an oak tree he will give you and acorn and when you cry out for a harvest he will give you a seed. The acorn and the seeds are already in your life; turning them to an oak tree and a field depends on how you develop the little things.

Many of us spend years running after "the big things" in our lives. We run after university degrees and bigger accomplishments when we have not taken care of smaller things like building strong relationships with people. The big things are important but the little things make the big things significant.

You can have a master's degree in a particular field and yet have no-one who wants to work with you because of your stinky attitude. On the outside you may look all together but on a closer look you may be full of cracks and leaks.

God has always honoured those who are faithful with the little things. God notes how well you do with the little that has been entrusted to you so that he can open the flood gates and bless you with more.

"Whoever can be trusted with very little can also be trusted with much, and whoever is dishonest with very little will be dishonest with much."
Luke 16:10

David was faithful as a shepherd boy and so he was given more. Joseph was faithful as a house servant, a prisoner and so he went on to be second in charge in all of Egypt. The widow was faithful in giving her last portion of her food to the prophet and her drums and those of her neighbours were filled to capacity with oil and flour.

If you are to become all that you can be, you've got to develop the little things already at your disposal. You don't have to look at what the next person has that you do not have. You can never reach success in your life using someone else's gifts and strengths. You have to look at what has been granted to you, it may be small but it's what you've got to work with.

Too many people are still waiting for someone to give them a leg up or to bless them in some way. If that's you, realize that you may be waiting for a long time while your life is wasting away. Start to carefully look at what you have, your relationships, your gifts, your opportunities. You might be at point A in terms of that gift or talent that is already in you, your job is to get to point B.

You can't blame your background, your family and your government forever. You've got to start building and that is done with one brick at a time. If you've taken care of your bricks or building blocks, the mansion will take care of itself.

What are the little things that you need to be developing in your life? What skills can you upgrade? Which relationships can you develop that will lead you to your dreams? What in your relationship with God needs attention right now?

Start developing the building blocks and see how the Castle of your dreams takes care of itself as a result.

WHAT CAN I LEARN AND APPLY?:

casting
your
vision

One movie which made a huge impact on my life is *Pay It Forward*. In the movie Trevor (a nine-year-old student) had a dream, to create a world where people help each other without expecting anything in return but pay it forward to others in return. He had to put a plan to it and Pay It Forward was the result and it reached across the USA.

If he had not acted on his dream, his desire to change the world would have remained just that - a desire without a clear vision and a plan.

Another movie which had a big impact on me was Patch Adams (based on a true story) starring Robbin Williams. It is a story about a man in his forties who admitted himself to a mental hospital and while there started to help the sick inmates. At that point he realized if he became a medical doctor and used his humour, he could really help people at multiple levels. In spite of his age, he enrolled at a medical school. What pushed him was a clear vision of where he could be, what he could do and the significance his life would make on others.

Dreams are achieved because of a clear vision. In other words, dreams which become a reality are the ones with a clear direction. A vision is a picture in one's mind of what the future looks like once the dream has been achieved; what will be different and what will be better as a result of the dream.

Vision is your map of your final destination and once you know this, getting there becomes much easier. In casting your vision you need to ask yourself:

- Where do I want to go?
- What do I want it to look like?
- How do I want to get there?
- When do I want to arrive by?

A vision is a statement of what your finished product looks like. This statement needs to be so clear that when someone asks you about it you need to be able to share it without having to read two pages from your diary.

Take time to write your vision today. These exercises might help you in doing just that:

Exercise 1:

Imagine you had all the resources you needed, what would you do and how would that change things? In other words how would you use all you had to make a difference in the world, your country or community? (Use a pencil)

_____

_____

_____

_____

_____

_____

_____

_____

_____

Exercise 2:

Picture yourself at your funeral. No-one else can see you but you can see all the people who have gathered to pay their last respects. You can see all your friends, family and members of your community. As each one stands up write down what you would like them to say about you and about your life. (Use a pencil)

_____

_____

_____

_____

_____

_____

_____

Now I want you to take time to write your vision statement combining statements from both the above exercises. Your Vision must be about what you will do and the person you will become as a result. Try to limit your Vision to a few concise sentences or paragraphs.

MY VISION IS

_____

_____

_____

_____

_____

_____

Many dreams remain dreams because we fail to put plans to them. By now you should be much clearer about your dream and your vision and how they tie into your purpose for being on earth. What follows now is another strategy to make your dreams a reality rather than just a wish-working out a plan.

All accomplishments in life happen when you take the first step. It doesn't have to be a large one. It just has to get you moving. Small steps will get you moving towards your dreams, until, one day, you realize you are there. You might not know or have the full plan of how you going to reach your dream but you have to write down your first step as well as some that follow after that.

"A journey of a thousand miles begins with but one step." –Chinese Proverb

Now that you are on the road to realizing your God-given dreams for your life realize that the most important step is the first one. What is the first step you might ask? It is very simple and most people miss it.

Your first step is putting together a plan. Jesus spoke often about the importance of planning and counting the cost before you start building your dream. He referred to the king going to war who sends spies ahead to check out the opposition to see whether his own army can hold ground. If the army that is coming against the king is much bigger than what his army can stand, he sends an envoy to negotiate terms of peace. Jesus also spoke about the builder who starts building without counting the cost and cannot finish his tower for the lack of resources.

Planning is more important than the actual building process. Without planning the actual building might end up looking much worse than the picture you had in mind when you started.

Most of us spend more time planning our holidays or studying the TV Guide than we do planning for the direction our lives are taking.

You need to set time aside to work on your plan for your God-given dream to be realized. You need to dedicate serious time for thought and meditation as you listen to what God is leading you to do with your life. A few years back I decided to take time out and seek God's direction for my life. I decided to take some time to listen first and so I went on a silent retreat. This was a very difficult thing for me to do because I love talking; I always have something to say.

Going on a silent retreat meant that I had to listen more - I read the Bible and silently allowed God's word to speak into my life. As the weekend went on ideas started to flood my mind as it became clearer what I needed to embark on. God started to show me ways that my life can make a significant and real impact in this world.

This time away from the rush of life allowed me to put a plan to my dream with God's guidance. Your strategy may differ but the principle still stands: Setting aside time to plan for the future will guarantee you a successful future!

WHAT CAN I LEARN AND APPLY?:

seizing
opportunities

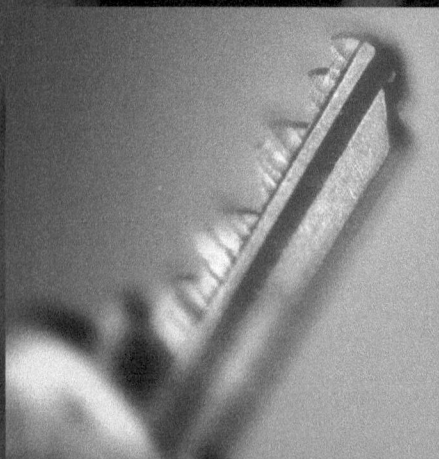

Most of us have heard the expression "Opportunity Knocks". At first glance this statement catches our attention and even excites us, to think that opportunity will come and knock at my door.

But in reality many of us find it hard to believe that opportunities come to knock at our doors. The truth is opportunity can and often does come knocking but often we are not equipped to recognise it.

In today's world opportunities abound regardless of what you may think or believe, the only problem is that opportunity often comes in overalls and looks like work. Opportunity is not the same as luck as some of us like to see it; it's actually work that brings us to the realization of our dreams. Often you hear people say "He was at the right place at the right time and that is why he is so successful." People will use these statements to explain away other people's success. The reality is those who succeed are the ones who seize opportunities.

Joseph seized the opportunity while he was a slave alongside other house-slaves. It was his work which set him apart from others and presented him an opportunity to be head of Pottipher's household. I have found my previous work has often landed me opportunities I never would have dreamed of. Through my service on a mission team in The Salvation Army, I got an opportunity to travel with the YFC International team and work with youth in Germany, the United Kingdom and the United States. Through this exposure of international ministry I landed an opportunity to direct The Salvation Army's youth work in Southern Africa for a few years. And on and on my story goes - as I was faithful to the opportunities which presented themselves so bigger opportunities knocked at my door.

Often people ask me how I got to be where I am today considering my background. My answer is I have learned to seize opportunities as they come. It all starts with the simple things, for me it was taking the opportunity to use the library in my rural school while others enjoyed the short-lived pleasures of a lunch break.

Here is another principle for activating your potential:

Seize the opportunity of a lifetime in the lifetime of that opportunity!

Opportunities have lifetimes; they do not last forever, you need to grab them while they are available to you. Right now there are opportunities that might be presenting themselves to you, they might come in the form of hard work, but if you take them it will change your future. As I look back at my life I am thankful for the opportunities God has presented to me but I thank him more for the ability to see them for what they were.

What Opportunities Knock?

_____

_____

_____

_____

_____

_____

_____

_____

_____

_____

_____

_____

_____

_____

_____

_____

WHAT CAN I LEARN AND APPLY?:

CHAPTER 20

making
every day
count

One of the greatest influences in my life has been the writings of wise men and women who have unpacked concepts that have enabled me to succeed. One of these men is John Maxwell through his many books on leadership and successful living. In one of his books *TODAY MATTERS* he touches on the importance of making each day count.

Failing to recognize the importance of each day in activating and living our God-given potential would be a grave error. It was Albert Einstein who said: "Time is the stuff that life is made of." Our lives are made of todays. Today is all that we are guaranteed of and it is in today that we can make decisions that will change our tomorrow. Tomorrow is not guaranteed and yesterday is gone forever; the only place I can make a difference is today.

Our lives become a success when we live our lives fully today. We bring honour to God by choosing to live for him today. What I did today matters in terms of who I'll be tomorrow. Life is a series of todays and a life that is significant on this earth is the one lived as if today is what matters most.

In this world we seem to live for tomorrow; constantly waiting in quiet desperation for the better days ahead. The problem with this kind of living is that we spend our whole lives in waiting. Waiting for that right opportunity to come our way before we start doing anything with our lives. Waiting for someone to validate us before we believe in ourselves. Waiting for the right climate and the right conditions before stepping out in faith.

The problem with waiting for your ship to come in is that you do not know when it's going to come in ...you might have missed it already. Isn't much better to look at each day as presenting you with a brand new opportunity to live now and make a difference today? Life that is fulfilled and significant regularly asks: "What can I do today to make a difference, to impact someone else's life, to live out my faith!"

To make each day count we need to be intentional about living in the now. When we are intentional about making each day count we become aware of what we spend our time doing and where that is leading us. If I seek spiritual growth and intimacy with God and those around me I will be intentional about making time for God and others today. If I want to succeed in my studies and my personal development I will be intentional about learning today. If I want to succeed in my business and career I will be intentional about doing all that I am required to do to succeed today.

It is every day that I activate my potential, it is every day that I am becoming the person I am meant to be. It is today that I fulfill my God-given purpose for living. Every day I must live according to the vision and the dream that God has for me for my dream will only be realized when I have lived fully today.

As you push on to activating your God-given potential here are some ways you can make each day count.

- Set aside time to spend with God today
- Decide what you'll focus on today
- Set aside time for the important tasks you need to do today
- Set aside time for the important people in your life (family, friends, etc) today
- Take care of your body, mind and soul (eat well, work well, learn and rest) today
- Plan for tomorrow today
- Keep your commitments today
- Have fun and enjoy life today
- Live in such a way that you'll have no regrets about today

If you take just one thought from this book I hope that it is the understanding that life is all about how you choose to live. You can choose to take a back seat and allow life to happen to you or you can choose to live fully as you were meant to be. I choose to live fully with an understanding that God has given me everything I need for a full life in Him. I choose to be actively involved in the direction that my life is taking and continually entrust to God's leading. I am not a victim but I am more than a conqueror through Christ Jesus who gives me strength and so are you!

What Have I Learned?

WHAT CAN I LEARN AND APPLY?:

www.ingramcontent.com/pod-product-compliance
Lightning Source LLC
Chambersburg PA
CBHW060133050426
42448CB00010B/2110